HOW GROSS, MY SÉANCES

How Gross, My Séances

Published by Plays Inverse Press
Pittsburgh, PA
www.playsinverse.com

ISBN 13: 978-0-9997247-9-8

Cover Art by Lauren Roche
Illustrations by Aidan Koch
Design by Tyler Crumrine
Printed in the U.S.A.

PLAYS
INVERSE

HOW GROSS, MY SÉANCES

A play in verse by
Jordan Chesnut with
illustrations by Aidan Koch
published by Plays Inverse Press
of Pittsburgh, PA in 2023

Prologue

Wastewater Treatment Facilities as the Greek Underworld

I stand underneath a sculpture of the planet, a paint-chipped replica. I can hear the Willamette River, home to the Kalapuya, Chinook, and Clackamas. A tributary of the Columbia, it passes through the Willamette Valley in Oregon. Here, along the walking trail, distances between celestial bodies in our solar system are scaled to mileage. Behind a tall, barbed, chain-link fence next to Uranus is a wet well, also called a sewage pumping station.

May 25, 2015
Noah has been missing for over three months.

Like watching a river's current, searching for a Missing person decomposes linear time. Events collage and blur out of context and out of sequence. The unknown battles with the known: *What if he reappears, but unrecognizable, unrelatable? What if he doesn't want to be found?*

May 30, 2015
I received a call from R… Noah's sister. They found a body in the sewage pumping station. At first, they thought it was a pile of blankets.

I am not writing Noah's story. I am writing about grief. Every experience of grief is as unique as the individual who passes away. In his wake, Noah left a world populated by his imagination; for a while, we shared this world, a mandalic, hand-strung paper mobile. Family and friends searched for three months before he was found, and we never determined how or why or where he left. I can only reach towards his departure, but by reaching, I part the curtains; through theatre, I cast and enact another kind of search. Is there anything remaining to be found? I allow multiplicities, negations, and divergence from a simplified, palatable, or logical narrative. With my finger, I feel what is growing through the cracked surface.

In Toni Morrison's essay "The Site of Memory," she writes of the flooding of rivers:

"Floods" is the word they use, but in fact, it is not flooding; it is remembering. Remembering where it used to be. All water has a perfect memory and is forever trying to get back to where it was. Writers are like that: remembering where we were, what valley we ran through, what the banks were like, the light that was there, and the route back to our original place. It is emotional memory—what the nerves and the skin remember as well as how it appeared. And a rush of imagination is our "flooding".

There are some memories that rise easily to the surface, and others that hide deep in my body, inaccessible. Before his memorial, I pulled a card from a deck. Of all things, it told me about the Chinese proverb of the frog in the well. Later, I learned that in a wet well, solid and liquid wastes are separated in a process known as primary treatment. Next, contaminants break down bacteria during secondary treatment. Then chlorine, nitrogen, or phosphorous is used to kill the remaining bacteria.

The Milky Way is named in English after the Latin, *Via Lactea*. Elsewhere, it is referred to (in translation) as The Way of the Birds; The Silver River; The Ganges of the Aether; River of Heaven; Field of Stars; Sea of Milk. Alongside two of his family members, I poured the remainder of Noah's ashes into the Mackenzie River, in a forest east of the Willamette where he was found.

June 2, 2015
My biggest fear is that he suffered or was afraid at the time of his death. A family friend told me, those of us left behind suffer loss. We are the ones who suffer.

Grief is the afterlife. While walking across the Charles Bridge in Prague, Franz Kafka hallucinated the bodies of civilians floating down the Vltava River as if it was momentarily transposed by the Styx. The movement of water in a river resembles the movement of grief—the changes in its depth, the multidirectional pathways of the current, and the closure as it flows into the ocean is metaphorical and cathartic. What happens to an archetype, like a river, when we are reckoning with ecological catastrophes, such as pollution and drought? Or when a river's passage is altered by the built environment through sewage pipes, irrigation canals, and drainage?

One of the last times I saw Noah he read to me from *The Last Days of Socrates* on the porch of his house. I still have the copy—weathered and with whole pages underlined in pencil. He told me about the Phaedo, and he especially loved the idea that learning is remembering. Remembering where we used to be and forever trying to return. In Greek mythology, the river Lethe is the river of forgetfulness and concealment.

There is a difference between forgetting and concealing. While the events may remain unknown, Noah's death was publicly visible, and his life was protected. Meanwhile, there are countless acts of targeted aggression, state-sanctioned violence, and degradation of individuals through carceral punishment that remain concealed to the greater public. A concealed death requires its community to assume the burden of reconciliation in tandem with, or in lieu of, memorial. Part of the very problem of contemporary political life is that not everyone counts as a subject. This is a play about the flooding of pipes as a choreographed act.

In the Phaedo, Socrates states, *The real earth, viewed from above, is made of twelve pieces of skin, variegated and marked out in different colors. Beneath, in the hollow places, the land is connected by unceasing subterranean rivers.* The rivers flow together at Tartarus and flow outward again; I imagine them flowing through a body: the rivers are physiological and hydrological.

The body is in bed. The body is on an operating table. The body is wounded, or it is a wound. Or the body isn't there, but instead, there is an indentation of a body in the sheets. A floodplain is restored to accommodate a river's need to remember. After the flood, islands and channels appear—what was lost in the reconsolidation of memory? It clots after it is stitched up, but what sensation is unfelt by the scar tissue? When I lift my head from my pillow my life bifurcates and flows away from his. He is gone. Ashes mix with sediment. *One of the penalties of an ecological education is that one lives alone in a world of wounds;* or, it is to live with the seemingly impossible task of determining relation in a world of wounds.

In wastewater treatment, when the process is complete, if the treated water meets regulatory standards, it is released to nearby water bodies. How are reports of discriminatory violence treated prior to resurfacing? The systematic separation of subjects by their identity is known as primary treatment. Next, the breakdown of culpability in media reports to defer responsibility—so we may remember to forget—is secondary treatment.

In July, on my way up north to Noah's memorial, I wrote: *The effects of drought are everywhere—trees are falling over from thirst.* Or, is it true that, if someone is denied long enough, they can believe they don't exist?

Water, water everywhere, / and not a drop to drink.

Character Descriptions

FLESH	A patchwork that wrinkles, sags, folds, oozes, and gashes open. It has slits and sometimes perspires. It is tattooed, scarred, picked at, prodded, stretched, renounced, oiled, stroked, enjoyed, detested. It is our landscape for the play.
GUTTERSLUT	Intuition, or the feelings themselves. She moves between memories and was born from a teardrop formed before the river became what-formerly-was, and Noah left his physical form. She is the avatar for the Narrator in the post-collapse world of grief.
NARRATOR	Logic, or rational thought. She is also nostalgic and remorseful. She writes at a suspended desk and pretends to direct. She is at odds with the Technician, whose implement at times becomes confused with her own.
STATUES	The Ensemble of Statues is a chorus. They are old marble relics and remind us of the hierarchies of love, desire, saviorism, memorial, and pursuit. However, they are weathered and wisened in their passage. Like Euripedes' Helen says, "If only I could shed my beauty and assume an uglier aspect / The way you would wipe color off a statue."

RIDING	A mother. She calls the Narrator and Gutterslut through a memory—the reception is fuzzy with static and arrives in the conjuring of a kitchen, which temporarily hovers on the shoreline between the manta ray and melancholic willow tree.
TECHNICIAN	Tattoos the Flesh, our memoryscape. He sleeps in the wound (his cave), and is not antagonistic, but postures as evil. In his bitter reclusivity we are reminded of the common suffering that occurs in the face of love and loss—the impossible wish to hold things in place, as they are, forever.
FISHERMAN	Baits his line on the shoreline of the River-That-Formerly-Was in the post-collapse world of grief. He wears suspenders. He is a shriveled paper scrap, a personification of patience amidst the ache; the simple act of casting out, and tempering longing in the wake.
SNAKE	Knows the movement of subterranean rivers, as they run, through the body. Narrates the interior.
FROG	A child of the subterranean. The Frog once resided in the bottom of the well, the deepest pits of Tartarus, or the sewage pumping station. It warns us of narrow-mindedness, because once the Frog had no idea what was outside of its well until one day, a turtle came along and told of the great wide world and big beautiful ocean. But when this particular Frog finally left its well, it realized that the River-That-Formerly-Was had been so polluted that the waters of the world no longer could be.

ROSE	A tattoo that performs in place of Noah during a date.
MERMAID	A tattoo that performs in place of Noah during a fun time swimming.
JOHNNY CARSON	Popular host of *The Tonight Show*.
CHRIS	A member of the Afterglow. Chris wears a pink hoodie and rests in a wheelchair with a respirator, and sings. The wheelchair doubles as a boat or vessel of some sort.
AFTERGLOW	The Ensemble of Afterglow is at times a disembodied point of light, a constellation to track. At other times they are embodied as the disavowed. They are a transposition of the Ensemble of Statues. The Afterglow alludes to the Statues, not as opposites, but as a refraction. What changes, or is altered, in the passage from one medium and into another? The movement of Afterglow teaches us about survival.

NOTE: The Flesh must not be one solid color, but show a variation of colors and textures.

Set Descriptions

A body is a world. The play takes place on a body. There are three primary sets:

The main locale is downstream along a river shoreline. This is where the Fisherman dwells. What is inside is reflected outside and the Fisherman is at the border of inside and outside. The river is a river of flesh, a river of sewage, and on the shore is a red bucket, a deceased but animate manta ray who whispers prophecies, a melancholic willow tree, washed-up debris, and a young couple approaching second base in a dusty clump of grass. The Fisherman casts his line while Gutterslut skips stones. The Narrator often writes on a platform above the scene. Occasionally, a memory of a kitchen in a former house with raspberry wallpaper and a home telephone is conjured on the shoreline. The Narrator lowers partway down to occupy the memory, while Gutterslut partakes, but peripherally.

Sometimes, we travel upstream, to the mountain cave (wound) where the Technician lives. Here, he tattoos the Ensemble of Statues who reside in the statue garden and cemetery nearby. The Technician's cave is adjacent to a tributary of the river of flesh, river of sewage, and some say he is a main pollutant. The walls drip, drip, drip while he swivels in his chair under a framed reproduction of *The Poet* by Pablo Picasso, and operates a remote controller to fly his drone downriver to spy on the others. In one scene, the actor who plays the Technician is interviewed in the cave, which transforms into the set of *The Tonight Show* with Johnny Carson. The set accumulates dwarf palm trees, television lighting, and a loveseat.

When Gutterslut submerges into the river of flesh, river of sewage, and lowers herself into the body of grief, the shoreline inverts. Upon entering there is a sensation of slicing the viscous dermis and gliding through glassy water. Curtains of light, like bioluminescence, open. Matter forms beneath and through Gutterslut's movements. Shapes and textures emerge as the body conjures them, and dissolve again. Proprioceptive, she skates, headfirst or on the heel of her palm. Sometimes she is caught in an eddy, a clot in the blood, clogged like a fixation or a knot in the gut. Meanwhile, the Afterglow flickers while roaming the refracted world, as a spotlight. On occasion, it tumbles outward with sparks and becomes light embodied and in motion.

How to Read the Play

The "Flesh" is a conceptual, sculptural prop. It is variegated in color and texture, and contains tattoos and projections, sleeves and slits, folds, bags, gashes, and wrinkles.

Dialogue written side-by-side is read simultaneously as a chorus in conversational harmony or it obscures and interrupts. Since the reader cannot read the text simultaneously they must negotiate where to place their attention. Text shown in italics and right-justified, or anything written in italics, is stage directions.

Since the landscape of this play is a body itself, the performativity of [dis]embodiment is crucial. This is shown through movement, gesture, and dance. The sprawl of dialogue across the page is reflective of the bodies present. The numbered prompts scattered throughout are phrasings for dancers. In the scene titled *AUTOPOIESIS*, dancers must have complete agency in designing their response through improvisatory movement.

At the start of the performance, the audience will be encouraged to explore their full range of movement while engaging with the script or its enactment. (So, lean back in your chair, squat, close your eyes and stretch your mouth into several contortions, stick out your tongue, grab your genitals and yell, open your chest and take a deep breath in, or stand on your head. Whatever you do, allow your movements to extend whatever feelings that arise to the surface of your body…)

[Insert movements here.] Begin.

IN LIGHT OF A LOSS A WORLD IS CREATED

The Narrator stoops, wrapped in a jacket,
and presses against a current of streaming light;
the pages of her notebook detach and fly midair.
During a sudden calm, she halts and remembers.
Then, disoriented, she floods. Within ten beats,
stillness is depicted with an atmosphere of blue.
Feverish, she drops to the ground and draws a map.

[Insert the Narrator's map of
the River-That-Formerly-Was
here.]

NARRATOR

To the Audience.

Along the River-That-Formerly-Was
are maps of the solar system
to show the distance between planets
by foot. Next to Uranus
is the wastewater treatment facility.

And what is inside is always
reflected outside—isn't it?

The Narrator slumps asleep
and dreams

of a body transposed onto an undulating page.
Text spreads beyond the boundaries of the page
body

itself, seeping. As she sleeps, the Technician apparates
and adds his amendments: A dam. A wet well. A manhole. A
canal. A vast irrigation system. A leaky faucet.

His pen scratching translates inside her dream
as the buzzing of a tattoo gun. Meanwhile, her mind
shuffles memories, which twist, refract, and double—
animated outside of herself.

[Insert Technician's map with amendments here.]

When the dreams subside they etch an imprint on the earth.

The imprint of a body that has vanished. The imprint of the waters' rise etched in the floodplain, once it recedes.

The last departing drop of water becomes Gutterslut, and then

a stream of

tears that cry her into being—

that cry her

from the map and into

the first act.

ACT 1

THE FISHERMAN

The Fisherman crouches beside a river in the post-collapse world of grief. The manta ray mumbles and the willow tree weeps. The young couple in the dusty clump of grass slowly approaches first base. The Fisherman baits the hook and a cloud drifts past the sun. The surface of the River-That-Formerly-Was darkens. This is a river of grief. Grief like fish rot, heavy with sludge. After a rain, the sludge dilutes, awash on the surface with residue: sticky plastic bags, old tires, an empty sealed wine bottle full of doodled dicks on shriveled bits of paper.

He crushes cans, belches, notices the little things: infinitesimal ripples from a distant cargo boat before the freight finally passes and the high notes conjured by each glint of light.

The Fisherman casts out so his burden plunks below the surface of the water. The line drops and, like a nerve, travels up, until he feels a stirring in his chest.

FISHERMAN

Casts his line.

GUTTERSLUT

Paces the shore.

Anything?

FISHERMAN

Turns. Grunts.

Nothin' to eat.

GUTTERSLUT

Long pause.

I was planning on swimming
in the river.

FISHERMAN

Laughs. Spits.

Not in this river ya aren't.

Gutterslut and Fisherman look to the current.

Gutterslut picks up a stone and squats to skip it. She flicks her wrist and lets the stone spin, flying.

GUTTERSLUT

I'm here because of a phone call.

Lights dim.

Instantaneously, the river drains around a corner, not to leave, but to wait.

RIDING CALLS THE NARRATOR

In the center of a junked-up shoreline, a kitchen
is conjured as a life-size diorama, a tableau:

Raspberry wallpaper, a round wooden table with a bouquet of tulips,
a bowl of five ripe plums, a small marble counter with a sink, and
a house phone mounted on the wall next to hanging pots and pans.

The Narrator enters, busy, and when a phone calls she sits at the table.
Gutterslut hovers outside on the surrounding shore. Riding's voice
enters from above, omnipresent.

NARRATOR
Picks up the phone.
Hello?

GUTTERSLUT
Picks up the phone.
Hello?

Static cuts in and out of dialogue, obscuring.

RIDING

As audio.

Hello.

Static.

I hope you've been well.

Static.

I'm calling about Noah.

GUTTERSLUT

My fault. My fault.
What has been done that—

NARRATOR

Noah was my partner.
Noah was
Noah is my
No—

Movement of backspace.

Riding is on the other line—

his mom.

RIDING

Apparently he—

Static.

at night. He hasn't shown up—

GUTTERSLUT

Can't be amended.

NARRATOR

To the Audience.

At the point she called he had only been missing for a few days. We—No—

Movement of backspace.

Noah—No. He's—

RIDING

—and no one has heard from him for a few days now…

Static.

NARRATOR

To Riding.

I heard from Noah a few days prior.

GUTTERSLUT

I turned away.

I called him every day until—

I called him, but—

He responded, *alright... getting by...*

I knew he wasn't. For a long time, I—

I knew he wasn't. I knew he wasn't alright.

For a long time I—

I should have told you.

—someone.

I should have told someone.

It's my fault. I should have—

NARRATOR

To Riding.

I'll try calling others. Let me know
if you hear anything.

GUTTERSLUT

Do you see the afterglow?

The Narrator hangs up the phone. As a paper bird, the room folds into itself and migrates.

GUTTERSLUT REFLECTS ON THE PHONE CALL

Shoreline. Gutterslut paces downstream until finding a hole in the earth.
A grave? A bed? She kicks clods and watches the dirt crumble downslope.

Gutterslut speaks aloud as several speculative bodies,
shifting in tone and awareness.

GUTTERSLUT
By not knowing where the body went / we think of it more as undying.

maybe he went—maybemaybe, no.
He wouldn't,

go there.
just say it
already.

okay, fine. on his last night,
someone mentioned he had been reading a book— about a frog...

?!

(r u talking abt the
children's bk?)

((yeah—the one where the frog
jumps off the back of a turtle to risk
its life for the other animals, i think.))

AND HE RE-EMERGES CLUTCHING SILT IN HIS TINY FIST!
A NEW LAND IS BORN! THE ANIMALS ARE SAVED!

[All ignore.]

*Well, I've heard that Noah was researching
storm drains. Which explains my theory.*

What's your theory?

*He climbed down a manhole into
the storm drains and a black hole
inside the earth sucked him up
and splat him out on another planet.*
[SLURPING SOUND…

Half the group exclaims skeptical remarks or laughs.]

!!!You know, it's thinking like this
that denies the facts!!!

Oh yeah? What facts do you
think you know, anyway?

t h e r e a r e q u e s t i o n s n o t a l l o w e d t o b e a s k e d
t h o u g h t s n o t a l l o w e d t o b e t h o u g h t

And why *sooooo* ominous?

Well, "what is inside is reflected outside" right?
and if thinking and feeling are live processes
then maybe we can re-enliven him, or a path to him,
if we can just keep these processes afloat—

Titania, Oberon, Ariel, Miranda, Puck…*

*Uranus has twenty-seven moons
named after characters from Shakespeare's plays.

Where [WHERE?] do the dead [DEAD?] go when they're gone [GONE?]???
Do they live inside of us [AHHH!!!] and if so for how long?

*Uranus is the planet of risk, innovation—
he was willing to take risks to be close to the people
in his life. "I have nothing to hide," he said—

he was lost,
and no one
reached out.
no one
stopped
to say—*noah, you are acting distant,* or—
sit down. what's up? Tell Me Everything.

(I know that I wouldn'tuv left him alone the night he disappeared.)

You can't know what you would've done if you had been there.

((noah said,

i guess i need to be the frog.))

who told u that ???

((it doesn't matter.))

on the topic of manholes—

[uhoh…]

he was also interested in socrates' tartarus.

[nooo that's like
a fiery hell pit where canceled celebrities go…
are you sure you don't mean
the greek underworld in general???????????]

Um, wherever is full of spiraling, converging rivers…
y'know where the dead go and they get, like, all sorted out.

[sorted out?]

sounds like
storm drains…
isn't that where
sewage goes?

In Hades there is Acheron (river of woe),
the Cocytus (river of lamentation),
the Phlegethon (river of fire),
the Styx (river of unbreakable oath),

he was discarded—
don't say that!

either he became trash, refuse, or
he just refused.
refused what???

to be separate?

the "I" "thou" relationship can only happen with a body—
—how can we dance between I and thou in all its forms?

and the Lethe (river of forgetfulness).

replace rivers with sewer lines,
and "souls" with "shit."

debris,
runoff,
gray water....

ya, S-H-I-T
i don't want to talk abt this anymore.

he said he wanted to...

"blast off."

THAT'SENOUGH.

too late. too late.

it's too late.

he said it though!

he wanted to *BLAST off.*

DON'T SHOOT—

he had his backpack
all ready to go.

like he was finna jus run straight to the hills?

no like in case something happened, idk…

a catastrophe… environmental or interpersonal.

ok. like he needed to board a vessel?

an ark?

(for the flooding of his imagination.)

AND SAID TO NOAH—

don't be stupid.

5

4

3

2

1…

RAPIDLY BLOOMING OVERNIGHT

Upstream. A cave is near the tributary of the River-That-Formerly-Was, inside of which the Technician works diligently, half-hidden by a partition. Ambling near its mouth is the Ensemble of Statues. The Technician summons each Statue over one by one, and while they recline, he tattoos. Some welcome the act and others resist. The tattooing is not malevolent, but instead habitual and unquestioned. The Statues talk quietly about their own fracturing, until they notice the Audience.

STATUE 1
Maybe it won't make sense.

STATUE 2
Until you've lost someone yourself.

STATUE 3
The way a part of you rearranges,

STATUE 4
blooming rapidly overnight

STATUE 5
and then wilting.

STATUE 6
When the one you are closest to vanishes.

STATUE 6 & 7
I am who I love. I am how I love.

STATUE 8
No, you are a tattoo. We are all tattoos.

TECHNICIAN
I tattoo, I do you.

GUTTERSLUT

Sobbing profusely.

And I am mourning.

GUTTERSLUT

Excuse me?

Gutterslut stands under the willow tree,
while the Narrator lowers down from a platform above
and scribbles in her notepad.

NARRATOR

Ha! No. You're the avatar of my grief.

NARRATOR

I can't find him without you. I have lists, you know,
lists and lists of facts, quantitative and qualitative data, sure!
But I just rerun the same sad memories over and over again,
it's like, seriously redundant. Then I hit a wall that says
[Robot voice] "You cannot proceed any further," because yes,
we found his body, but what happened? How did he arrive
where he was going, and why? I swear he may have slipped
through a crack and for all we know he will return, come
back—

STATUE 1

Think of yourselves as the two sides—
reason and feeling. Order and expression.

GUTTERSLUT

Body (book).

NARRATOR

Mind (pen).

STATUE 2

A connection must be restored between the two
in this liminal space—

STATUE 3

Liminal, as in transitional, and
Limn, meaning to highlight, to suffuse or portray, illustrate.

STATUE 4

Which is to say, let us elucidate our ludicrous aliases, you know,
you and you and you, but illustriously. Lord, allow me
to earnestly labor in pursuit of all plausible worldlings
for this! Lamentable loss! And all the rest! Hallelujah, blah, blah, blah—

NARRATOR

I'm confused– are we mourning a death or searching for him still?

STATUE 5

Like a painting, our liminal world holds all potentialities simultaneously. He is dead and alive, victim and culprit, always and never—

ENSEMBLE OF STATUES

Singing.

I want the memory of me to be a happy one.

RAPIDLY BLOOMING OVERNIGHT, PT. 2

Suspended on the platform above the cave, the Narrator claps and shouts:

NARRATOR
Repeat the scene, recollect, begin!

Light shifts. The Technician takes off his sweater and then puts it back on. Meanwhile, the Ensemble of Statues shuffle across the stage to (nearly) align with their original placement in the previous scene—akin to the inaccuracy of a mental image, reconsolidating, doubling back on itself, a transposition…

STATUE 1
Maybe it won't make sense.

STATUE 2
Until you've been shuffled, rearranged,

STATUE 3
the way in which every memory slips out of focus,

STATUE 4

the picture emerges, sunwashed,

STATUE 5

inaudible. It is an urgency so luminous all boundaries erase

STATUE 6

when the one you are closest to vanishes.

STATUE 6 & 7

I am who I love. I am how I love.

NARRATOR

Louder!

STATUE 6 & 7

I am who I love. I am how I love.

STATUE 8

No, you are a tattoo. We are all tattoos.

The Technician blotches Statue 8 with a towel and she smears.

GUTTERSLUT
And I am morning.

NARRATOR
A late winter morning when he comes and the search
is over we will make breakfast and eat it on the porch:
Eggs and butter on toast, coffee with cream.

GUTTERSLUT
How many times can we rehearse,
it will never resemble—

NARRATOR
I can't find me without you all I have is him!

STATUE 1
Think of yourselves as many-sided—
Muck and leak.

GUTTERSLUT
Silt, or a supple response under skin.

NARRATOR
Frack, or excavate tirelessly with logic.

STATUE 2
And in this liminal space—

STATUE 3
Subliminal, the suppression of information.
Limb, meaning appendages of the body. Arms. Legs.

STATUE 4
Is there is a relation between what is inside
and outside? Rivers of grief, rivers of sewage.

STATUE 5
Only that I break and reconfigure my body and limbs so
the contamination held inside is visible from the outside.
This mutilation, a sacrifice of composure to be heard.

ENSEMBLE OF STATUES

Singing.

I want the memory of me to be a happy one.
I'd like to leave an afterglow of smiles when life is done.

The sound of water swells with the repetition of their song and washes all offstage.

ACT 2

PRACTICING ON THEIR OWN SKIN

Zoom out. Zoom way out until you can see the River-That-Formerly-Was from above. Look at your arm, thigh, or stomach. The Flesh is our landscape, as Gutterslut and lonely, lowly grief and its constituents continue to travel and traverse in search for the missing parts of themselves.

Keep in mind, Flesh is not clean. Flesh is desirous and self-shaming. Flesh is picked at, prodded, stretched, sloughed off. Flesh is the border between the body and the vastness of all beyond it. To inhabit one's flesh is the equivalent of toeing a steep ledge. The Flesh can be embodied or disembodied. Cast off. Burned down. Shunned. Discarded and sewn up. Dissoluted and strewn into a dream, entangled or enmeshed with another. Flesh is not one tone, but variegated, like "the many colors of the earth."

Each tattoo, an island, consolidating and reconsolidating meaning. It does both at once. It comes as a surprise when something so fixed appears to shapeshift. Just as, when we look in the mirror, we never see our same selves. Always misconstrued, distorted somehow.

The eye is a magnifying lens, and the mind becomes a pair of tweezers—
or worse, a retractor, dilator, or cutter. Or a pen can become a gun…
did you know this?

STATUE 1
Here, we begin and live in grief.
We begin and live on the body.
Spotlight on a lump of flesh,

Writhing!

STATUE 2
Time is not linear, but marked by passions.

STATUE 3
In the body of grief, memory will be represented as tattoos.
All that is left.

In the corner, under a spotlight, the Technician cleans his tools with a toothpick in mouth.

TECHNICIAN

Big flesh day today, friends. Flash only!
Hashtag remember forever hashtag inkdaddy.

STATUE 5

(The origin of flesh is shown here as two bodies
wrapped in a large swatch of gauze-like tapestry.)

STATUE 6

The nascent forms of love and loss move amorous,
amorphous, and unravel, writhing.

STATUE 7 & 8

A landscape of flesh.

TECHNICIAN

Here's an idea: my face tattooed on your ass? Hey—
relax, relax already it's a joke.

Sound of a tattoo gun.

STATUE 4

The gun, humming. Ink bleeds.

STATUE 5

The Technician leans down to wipe,
or lick, the blood.

Out of the Flesh emerges a bed inside of a wound.
Gutterslut folds into the scar tissue, and it absorbs her.
The Technician climbs inside the scar to lie with Gutterslut.

Lights off. All exit.

Lights on. Gutterslut lays alone.

Rain catches Gutterslut and carries her into the next scene. She floats along the surface of the river of Flesh, sees the Fisherman's hook, and passes its fang, gleaming. A whirlpool sweeps her ashore.

AN INVESTIGATION OF A TATTOO [BELOW COLLARBONE]

At the tributary, in the mouth of the cave. Dripdrip.
The Technician—a self-proclaimed master of his craft—tattoos a rose on the Flesh. He wipes his brow on his sleeve. Dabs blood. The Rose is drawn adjacent to a heart with an arrow. A "Mom" in script. The bloody heart smears across the collarbone where the Rose now drapes. Both are memories inked in memoriam. At this moment, the Rose is a stand-in for Noah, an instance of him temporarily conjured.

Gutterslut ambles along the shoreline until spying the Rose self-actualizing in the fog. She slumps beside the dewy flower, bereft, while the Technician dissolves into the background.

The Narrator speaks through the Rose while writing on a suspended platform above the scene.

ROSE

Performs through movement.

1. Divinates through the arrangement and rearrangement of bouquets. (A version of *he loves me, he loves me not...*)
2. Fantasy is a rose hedge. Expectations are the clippers found in the free box on the street corner. I don't say *my roses* because I want them to exist as free agents, sunbound;
3. but sometimes, we all want to own and be owned. Like a crush, they grow laterally from the stem, until their density and fervor demand passing remarks.

NARRATOR

Speaks down the left column.

In the rose garden he denied the fact.
It was our first date.

Spring is

sunlight and collarbone.
Unvocalized feelings undermined to save
face. My friend Claire arranging and rearranging
bouquets (and what if that
were a kind of divination.)

Why did I always

Defer.

GUTTERSLUT

To the Rose, reclined beside her.

Your shirt is ripped. I thought you said
you wanted to go out to dinner.

I don't know if you've noticed this yet,
but I constantly—

I'm unsure.

I think of how much I couldn't know then,

and the insecurities absolved
by mounting expectations and flattery.

I think of blossoming
and unfamiliar warmth.

Warmth speeding up
towards an end point.

I don't always trust myself, or what I feel,

but I want to spend time with you.

If only it were as easy as divinating
with bouquets, then I could tell us
where to go to dinner or—

name this warmth
out loud.

Aren't you cold
with all those holes
in your shirt?

ROSE

As herself.

Gutterwet.

The Rose seeps into its surroundings, coupled with a dinner receipt, olive pits, and a melted candle (objects haunted and out of place that would rather not explain their presence, but somehow made it here, too). Noah stands in the doorway. With my eyes I say Come Inside, but this iteration of him in the afterlife is only an idea, a memory… like a palindrome, or a wind-up toy, re-enacting our first date on the mat that says "Welcome" until I have no choice but to shut the door.

AN INVESTIGATION OF A TATTOO [UPPER THIGH]

Lawn sprinklers flood the sidewalks and fill a shoreline. Small waves wobble ashore from a passing tanker. The Technician crouches and tattoos a Mermaid on the Flesh. The Technician wipes his brow on his sleeve. Dabs blood. Fishrot. Ripple glints alongside the melodic, high pitch.

Gutterslut clumsily changes into her swimsuit underneath a towel and the Mermaid reclines and chain-smokes cigarettes, poised on the edge of the frame, or slung around the side of a thigh.

The Narrator views from above, and dictates aloud while writing.

NARRATOR

We would say it in a long drawl,
like bourgeois snobs sprawled on a rock
below an abandoned factory,
and we'd take drags—

GUTTERSLUT
Speaks to Mermaid.
UrrrrbaAAahhhn meeerrrmaaaiiiid.

Noah was the first person I met who'd swim
unabashedly in the river.

He'd throw all his clothes off at once like
a three-year-old. Never sexual.

Just free… at first glance.

I don't want
this constant

voice of judgement
I carry.

Both share the cigarette.

I'd rather not. Yeah, who knows
who is leering in the brush…

I don't want some…

brush-perv
checking me out.
Smiles.
You're right
I'd crush their skull
with my thighs
if I caught 'em.

As if my self-doubt fractured me
from a kind of knowing. Always
three steps to the left of myself.
Movement of a backspace.

Drags cigarette.

You have it easy.

Even when you are naked
you evade all connotations
of what it means to be exposed.

GUTTERSLUT, NARRATOR, and MERMAID
Simultaneously acknowledge.
Scales.

Gutterslut and the Mermaid look upwards. A pipe leaks sewage. The Afterglow stirs in the water. Gutterslut attempts to lift the glow above the sludge with two cupped palms. Meanwhile, the Fisherman's hook hovers. The Mermaid blows smoke at its bait.

At sunset, the Mermaid and Gutterslut drowsily stumble away, with their arms locked.

WE ELABORATED A SYSTEM

A Statue passes, sweeping sewage and cigarette filters offstage with a broom. We are somewhere in between limbs, in the liminal, a crease, a shadow, a question mark, directionlessness…

NARRATOR

When he went missing we elaborated
a system of thinking underground, collectively.

Gutterslut pushes through the underbrush. Car lights flash through branches. She pulls herself up. Phone conversations overlap—disparate voices speculate whereabouts and grow louder until drowning out.

ENSEMBLE OF STATUES

A mass. Pantomimes, in situ.

1. Transmits information (emotional) underground. I give and you receive, ad infinitum. This must be a community.
2. The community silences under the surveillance of clouds. Phone calls arrive nonstop with false reports—*I seen him, yawp.*
3. In the passing storm, communication dead circuits. (A friend is overheard bitterly stating, *He better not be dead after we have put all this effort into searching.*)
4. Distrust proliferates, gaseous, and we speculate in small groups while side-glancing across assumed distances.

The Ensemble of Statues are felled with a swing of lights,
and walk through the aisles of the Audience
to distribute "Missing" flyers, but instead of Noah's face
is an erasure of face… a smear, an absence of self.
Each Statue inquires of the Audience members down each row.

Have you seen him?

Have you—have you

seen—?

Do you feel and

where does the feeling reside?

A voice

releasing

its mind?

STATUE 1

Can we enact his leaving? Rehearse each possible outcome
of the night he left?

ENSEMBLE OF STATUES

1. The Ensemble of Statues swing-dance in pairs. Glassware slides from shelves and shatters.
2. In the sudden stillness, the lead collapses, deceased.
3. The follow kneels and shakes the lead.
4. Switch partners. Responsibility requires action, a response. Repeat step 3.
5. The lead rises. Their rising will be indicative of either A) a performative response to showcase compassion or B) a natural extension of one's devotion regardless of optics.
6. Repeat steps 1-5. Replace follow shaking the shoulders of the lead with—

    I. Mouth-to-mouth resuscitation.

    II. A head in a lap.

    III. One pair of hands on both faces.

Sound of a heart monitor. Siren lights.

No sound of a siren.

ENSEMBLE OF STATUES

Yell all together. Stomp feet.

No!

1. Hold flashlights, search for the body around flesh and through the audience, under chairs.
2. Rejoin on stage. Hold light under faces. Silent scream. All collapse to the floor.
3. Yell, "No!" with varying intonations, and turn flashlights off.

AN ATTEMPT AT CONTACT

Shoreline. Light undulates and refracts in late evening. The Fisherman casts out and sits on a bucket. Spits tobacco. Swigs beer. Freeway gray noise mixes with the tide and passing freight. He watches the young couple feverishly approaching third base in his periphery and pulls out the sealed bottle floating in his subconscious, breaks it open, and skims its shriveled notes. Ballpoint pen, faded. His mind wanders back to his ex, whose face now blends with the young woman that sells fruit popsicles in the parking lot on weekends. He kicks the broken glass aside and begs the willow to offer him one more fish before dark, before the sky turns red. He'll go to the market in the morning. He'll sling fish for cash to the tourists and tell them it's farmed. He'd never eat the meat himself, no way in hell. Have you ever seen the rivers in post-collapse?

Before he can reel in and cast out again, Gutterslut slips over, like oil pools up under a car at night, and makes a little rainbow in the drainage ditch.

Sound of a heart monitor. Gutterslut walks out and the Fisherman baits his line.

He looks over his shoulder to talk to Gutterslut.

FISHERMAN

A little drunk.

Yeren't as slick of a sluth as ya think.

Spits.

I no cuz I'm lookin fer someone too.
Suresasshell.

GUTTERSLUT

Oh ya? Who's that?

FISHERMAN

Hesitates.

Not x-zactly sure… But I'll no when I meet em.

GUTTERSLUT

How will you know? I mean, how does anyone know when they are in love?

FISHERMAN
Because I'll feel 'em before they surface.

Both pause to consider.

GUTTERSLUT
A single worm alluringly curled on the tip of your hook?

FISHERMAN
Like a fish!

GUTTERSLUT
Singing Celine Dion…

FISHERMAN
There's a tug before the breach.

GUTTERSLUT
I'm not mocking you.

FISHERMAN
The sky!

GUTTERSLUT
Wild horses. Rain ringing like bells.

GUTTERSLUT

Skips stone.

I keep getting stuck in the replayed memories,
The Narrator wants me to intuit some cause or series of events to either find him or rationalize her closure…
and meanwhile—

FISHERMAN

A great wind carries me across the sky.

Look, I don't have much to offer.

Long pause.

But you could do like me—
Keep baiting. Keep waiting…
yup, that sureasshell is one way to do it.

Pause. A knowing glance.

Or you could go
down,
and through…

GUTTERSLUT
Are you saying—

Snake emerges from a slit in the Flesh.

SNAKE
To travel in subterranean
water,
rife with contaminants,
in the leaky
conveyance of slump skins,
the slow,
sepulchral creep,
oiled slick, and on fire,
while half-asleep.

The Frog struts through a partition in the Flesh, and stands before them.

FROG

To the Audience.

Gutterslut picks up a stone and squats with her arm angled to skip the stone. She flicks her wrist and lets the stone spin.

Lights off.

The Afterglow skips upstream, while the Fisherman reels in, we follow the glint.

ACT 3

THE AFTERGLOW SKIPS

And the Afterglow "hello"s the whole way through.
"Screw this murk," it thinks, "it's so hard to see
where to land."

Yes, the Afterglow is sentient. It is not of one mind, but
multiples. If anyone understands the Afterglow,
it is the Frog.

The glint plunks upstream.

(*plunk*)

THE TECHNICIAN MAKES AN APPEARANCE ON *THE TONIGHT SHOW*

Upstream, in the cave beside a tributary, the set of The Tonight Show *is loosely reconstructed: fake dwarf palms, swivel chair, desk and loveseat are positioned beside film camera lighting.*

The Technician sits in the loveseat beside his interviewer, Johnny Carson, who is stationed behind the desk. Johnny asks the actor who plays the Technician a series of questions. They begin with playful jabs and jokes not pertaining to the story, which the actors improvise prior to the written text. The Audience applauds and laughs accordingly.

JC: You make me laugh, [Insert actor's name here]. Okay, so enough of the jibber jabber. Let's hear it—why is the Technician a tattoo artist?

T: I'll try to contain myself, Johnny, because, I'll tell you—embodying this character hasn't been easy. I had a conversation with my friend the other night about her experiences last year with chronic illness. In the past couple weeks, her phone broke and all of her photos from that time in her life were erased. She never backed any of it up to a Cloud. She panicked because the images helped her remember what she believed to be, a fuller account of her illness. This led us into a really fascinating discussion about transactional memory and our predisposition to isolate certain moments in order to construct a personal narrative around hardship.

JC: Or, on a larger scale perhaps, we allow our trauma to be the dominant story of ourselves…

T: Right! Look, I love tattoos. But since our play takes place on a body, and in that environment, I think that something in print, published, condensed, made permanent, concretized, stripped down to its most legible and marketable form may be reminiscent of a tattoo… In relation to memory and grief, it may be manifested as narratives of self-blame, reinforced by memories that tell us a single story of one's failed response and responsibility.

JC: So tattoos are like identity markers based on potentially false, or at least incomplete, conceptions of the self—right?

T: In the universe of the play, yeah, they're reminiscent of what you are describing. And I think it's important to note that, outside of this universe, tattoos are culturally significant. Like in Southern Morocco, brides paint their hands with henna before their weddings; and in Eastern Polynesia, Tā moko is the name for permanent body and face markings in traditional Māori culture, which are seen as an important status marker. One could say that the stigmatization of tattoos is a colonialist mentality that has roots in early British expeditions to the South Pacific led by European sailors who eventually created an expressive tattoo tradition of their own. But people around the world have taken part in various forms of body art for centuries. To be honest, I don't know much about it.

JC: Maybe just as important, too, is how these cultures you are describing recognize their bodies or selves as part of a larger whole… and tattoos help us visually interpret that relationship. Could you say more about what the tattoos mean for us here, in this text? In this world?

T: Yeah, definitely. I mean, we are always fluctuating, internally shifting and changing, so how do we align with a socially legible self-image? I would say, it's important to scrutinize outdated expectations about how we are supposed to perform—individually or collectively—as people. Ultimately, with tattoos in the "post-collapse world of grief," a tattoo is not stigmatized or negatively connoted as a *bad* memory or mistake; rather, if we see the body as a river, the tattoos are like the imprints of the self left behind when the channel drains or changes course. Therefore, tattoos pose a threat only when the protagonist sees an image as totalizing, or when they fail to recognize a single mark as a part of that much larger whole, as you mentioned.

JC: What about the Technician? Do you see examples of your character in the world outside this body of text?

T: Personally—and this is just me—I can see ties between my character and, for example, self-appointed "leaders" who demand walls to keep others out; self-actualizing within the permitted confines of state surveillance like social media platforms; the marketing of identity by consumer brand names; or the rapidity of news reports and duration of public attention. The list goes on. In any case, it's these aforementioned social trends or public figures that create single narratives around certain populations and, in doing so, galvanize violence. We can do it to people we love, too, or ourselves… It is just as dangerous to insist on elevating someone for their assumed virtue as it is to continuously condemn them for their alleged misdeeds.

JC: I think about each time someone asks me the story behind one of my tattoos. It's often the same question. They want to know what it means to me… i.e., the significance. I've trimmed my response down to its boilerplate, like a three-word sentence, and the more I repeat this summation the more I doubt its validity. In all honesty, I do wonder what truly compelled me to make an image a permanent part of myself. My ideas and feelings and sense of self change almost every day. Oftentimes, the tattoos are merely decorative, and over time, I forget I have them at all.

T: Now I have a question for you.

JC: Ok.

T: In writing about what we don't know, when does a pen become a gun? And when it does, what happens as a result?

In response to Johnny Carson's question, the following poems apparate as ghosts—multi-limbed, faintly incandescent, and immense as clouds—and each one migrates downstream to haunt what has already occured.

THEORETICAL TATTOO #261

In the park on the wet grass. I didn't feel
heard or
seen so
I left my journal in your room. You stopped
by to return it. *Did you read*
anything? And you said no. It is
not mine
to read, you said. And I felt
you behind a wall;
now I write as if to break it. "Have you noticed how dimensions of a thing will change
when the body moves or the skin ages?" I say while admiring this tattoo.

THEORETICAL TATTOO #3,258

It became easier to ignore you when your expressions were un-
familiar. And the more I pushed away,
the less familiar you became
and the more
expressive of what appeared to me, uncharacteristic and so
(I convinced myself) necessary to avoid. Desperation is a quick passage to ignite
distancc, which hid you from many of us. "This tattoo?
Most people
never see
this tattoo
I can't
even see it
without
pivoting
like *this*
in front of
a mirror."

Gutterslut and the Narrator replace Johnny Carson and the Technician in their seats on The Tonight Show. *But rather than positioning themselves as interviewer and interviewee, they assume the positions of therapist and client. The Narrator lies down at first, but slowly rises to stand as she speaks…*

NARRATOR/GUTTERSLUT

As they speak, the Narrator and Gutterslut temporarily fuse, overlapping, entwining, and then separate again.

Who am I really searching for?
Is this all self-serving?
Do I want to give him support or do I feel as if it's owed by me?
Would my love and support even stand a chance of bringing him back?
What would it look like? What would I say?
What would I bring him back to?
To an idea of who he is supposed to be?
To an idea of what we could have been
and what his life is for? Who am I to decide, and
either way, is it him I am searching for
or what he represented?
His willingness to give everything for nothing.

Am I chasing his commitment to building another world
to disavow that commitment for myself?
Am I hiding inside of him?

Suddenly fissured, they continue speaking.
Their words, muddied in simultaneity, or interruption.

NARRATOR
Talks to self while writing.
And the tattoos are fragmentary.
So is the recorded narrative.

Movement of backspace.

I try to fix
what I know

in place. It's always
skewed, faded, warped,

GUTTERSLUT
Gestures to self while speaking.
How is a tattoo akin to a memory,
akin to a memorial,

akin to

a mark,
an othering,

a division,
a difference?

a caricature
of my own subjective

lens,
superimposed

by the present
each time it is conjured

again.
In drawing

from memory
I exaggerate

a new
deficiency—

the eye,
placement

It's like if the Signifier took his or her
Signified
out on the town…
to meet his boss
or mother…

We want someone to stay inside the lines
to fill a role.
Hello, I'd like you
to meet my Signified.

Imitates a greeting.
Hello! How do you do?
Like memory,
a partner changes
shapes over time. Their presence

must be constantly reintroduced, allowed to
expand,
contract,

of a hand, tone
of what was spoken…

Gutterslut is my avatar, I mean,
an extension

of my past
flaws and actions.

An emblem
of my psyche, the feeling

body, maybe,
built to follow

Noah the night
he left.

change form,
double back,
and contradict. Like me,

I am the Narrator's avatar, but
I don't always extend
her logic. Sometimes, I—

project the alternative.

I *am* the feeling that may
undermine logic.
Maybe,

I regret less. Maybe, I wouldn't have followed…
Noah the night
he left, in hindsight.
How is *to allow* different than *to turn away*?

Turns to Gutterslut.
No. You would never. How could you?

You're right. No.
I said that out of fear, the unknown,
you know, I would have—

If you don't want to find him,
then we never will.

Well, whether I would or wouldn't have
been able to follow him the night
he left, and whether I did or didn't
try to hold him in place
for so long before he vanished,
I can keep looking now. Regardless.
If that's what you think is best. I'll try.

You need to want this as much as—

I do! I need to know where he went,
it's true, maybe we can still—
Quiets…
Blast off.

Don't shoot.

The Statues enter and circle around the Narrator and Gutterslut on set, both fall silent.

STATUE 1

As she listens to Gutterslut and the rest speak, the Narrator realizes…

STATUE 2

How the logical mind can confine the intuition…

STATUE 3

Yet, she questions this dichotomy. She wonders…

NARRATOR

Is it as simple as body and mind? What about speech? To speak is, itself, a bodily act; but to speak up or out shatters the distinction, although—

STATUE 1

Repeat. Explain.

NARRATOR

Is it as simple as body and mind? What about speech?
Meaning, speech draws lines over the body. To name
may incidentally redact or override a physical act.

GUTTERSLUT

But they are connected, *our mouths won't work*
without our minds.

NARRATOR

Maybe speaking urgently would have saved him.
These words are arriving all too late—

GUTTERSLUT

Or I can name "my well," "my tomb," "my home,"
and by doing so, I can go—

Gutterslut finds a piece of chalk on the ground and outlines a body midair. It hovers. The Technician fades in and out of center stage, an apparition, his face floating and transposed behind the outline. The Narrator and Ensemble ignore all of it and instead reference scripts to debate lines.

STATUE 5

So speech and the body are inseparable,
but incongruous. And, by naming
herself the Narrator,

STATUE 6

she inadvertently prioritizes her stance,
her logic, over Gutterslut, the intuition...

STATUE 7

Feeling. The grief itself, unbound from any moral
or otherwise logically defined complications…

GUTTERSLUT

I have morality…!

STATUE 8

That, as words may illuminate or conversely
overwrite a viewer's experience of a painting,

STATUE 1

her causality and orchestration from above
distorts the inner workings of this world…

STATUE 2
The afterlife. Sludge and sluttage.

NARRATOR
I project my experience onto her, and in doing so, I silence her.

Gutterslut and the Narrator turn towards each other;
the latter shakes with recognition.
One Statue gasps,
another exasperatedly faints,
and a third checks her phone.

The Snake enters down a pole, a centerfold,
a trumpet solo, a highway flare seen from a hedge
maze. And the Ensemble says

5

6

7

8—

SNAKE

Well, do you want to go?
Down sewers,
beneath the dermis,
deeper…

Laughs. Glitches.

where your answer
rests,
sequestered_realize.docx

Well?

Do you want to?

Down sewers,
beneath the dermis,
deeper… where your answer goes?
Finally, after all this searching you will,
you will beyourown. You will be
your own personalized answer.
Well? Do you?

Laughs.

Deeper into the body?
Here, nothing has a name
so you can call it what you'd like. Input your destination into the Body
Search System and I will guide you. You. Well?
Deeper. You are sequestered,
here, nothing. Your destination. Whatever
you bring back
to the surface
will be taken from you. Extracted.
Filtered.
Processed.
Bleached. Whatever you
realize. Your answer. Will be used against you. If you put your mouth on my.
Well, my tomb. Swallow it. Casket.

Unless, you choose to stay, of course.

TECHNICIAN

Well. Tomb. Home. *La fin.*

GUTTERSLUT

Mouth. Pussy. Corpus. Roll credits.

SNAKE

Snake in the grass. Shhh…
How do I get under
that flesh? Shhh...

STATUES

Sing like jeering, or like encouragement.

Slutslutslust lust.
Go on you slut.
Slutty.
Gutter.
You can do it slut.
Slut, we believe in you.
Yas, slut!

Repeat and trail off.

As Gutterslut slowly begins to descend with the Snake the others remain above. Sewage rushes in. The Flesh inverts. Lights flicker.

The Snake dances insatiably.

Gutterslut tentatively meditates.

The Frog moodily plays the piano.

The Afterglow, elusive, sinks deeper…

VIEW FROM THE INSIDE

Slowly, the shoreline inverts. All is blue, wet, and pulsating. Gutterslut has dropped to the other side—slipped inside the body whose surface we have been traveling along. She now sees grief from its cavernous depths. Murky and subterranean.

Here, everything responds with touch. Here, answers to the haptic, sensorial. Responds and is responsive. Moves easily. Is intertwined. Water dripdripdrips in a hollow space. Walls move, blue, the Flesh undulates. Veins emerge, blood flows.

A tattoo bleeds, inverted as a mirror image, an unexpected paid programming visible through the viscous depths in the body of grief.

TATTOO #5,881

Near the rose garden we swam
beneath
        the future site of his body. Was there a moment
        he or I or someone else
        could sense this,   like a change of current
                                        a few strides away? I say,

"This tattoo eddies straight down into a well
where a frog patiently waits, laughing."

MUCKMUCK AND LEAK HELLOS

GUTTERSLUT

Anyone here?

Touches the glint which scatters into pointilations of light.
When the light scatters it shapeshifts to bodies.

The Afterglow oscillates between its lit, autonomous form and its embodied, disparate parts.

AFTERGLOW

Each is underlit as they speak.

Here

Here!

Here…

(Here.)

1. The Ensemble of the Afterglow dance in pairs. Glassware slides from shelves and shatters.
2. The follow is shot by the neighboring lead.
3. The lead crouches and shakes their follow.
4. Switch partners. Responsibility requires action, a response. Repeat step 3.
5. Lead rises. Their rising will be dissociative, and after they are standing again they will be reassured by someone else that nothing, in fact, happened at all.
6. Repeat steps 1-5. Replace lead shaking the shoulders of their follow with—
    I. Filming the act of shooting.
    II. Each lead attacking the shooter of their follow.
    III. Taking the bullet to the chest.
    IV. Create a human checkout stand, and pass through one-by-one.

Police lights.

AFTERGLOW
Yell all together. Stomp feet.

Stop!

1. Hold flashlights, search for the body around flesh and through the audience, under chairs.
2. Rejoin on stage. Hold light under faces. Silent scream. All crumble to the floor.
3. Yell "Please let me be!" with varying intonations, and turn flashlights off.

THE FROG AS PRESCIENCE, POLLUTED

A grief river contaminated by forgetfulness, concealment.
It pulls in the external pollutants until it becomes uninhabitable,
undrinkable. This murk is thick. River of flesh, river of sewage
(composed of bodies stripped of speech, discarded, and made obsolete).

The Frog, prescient, tosses cut flowers.

FROG
Tossing cut flowers.
I, swimming. Submerged. I, river.
My body chiseled flat, stoic;

pickpick, thumb, let spin.
Prescience. I, not-all-at-once,

but in successions, soul amasses
like a dress around the ankles

and body is sloughed asunder
cotton or buried under

the muddy shore. Soulless. No
breathing. Taptap. Shush.

Buryit. Buryit. Buryit.
Who says, sullen?

I, cellular, absorb
arsenic, pesticides, solvents. I,

pointilations composing
and submerged.

Where (glowing) is our guide?
I, downstream cadmium, mercury,

zinc, copper, lead, and I,
cyanide. I,

Tone shift to the didactic.
(Only performative gestures

exist now, the People say: Justice is only entertained out of the fear of
personal retribution but doesn't that make any pursuant results unjust?)
Shifts to restore the former tone.

Septic and seep of storage
tanks, waste, and fertilizers. I,

landfill, easy-does-petrol. Hello?
Here we are!

I, the family evacuated.
I, the product of the family
evacuated. I, afterthought. I, hindsight.

I, so-called, composite, infectious
amalgamation of the "I"

themselves, sticky, plastic, plural.
(Who believes in a we, a plural now anyhow?)

Smelters, concentrators, processors
along the crick. Industrial

carrier, the river. The I. The ruckus
that hardly ensues, suchandsuch a shame.

Waterfunk. Watersludge.
Muckmuck and leak. This, I.

Meanwhile, Gutterslut follows the stones,

spinning… into the gradual
loss of a center, water draining, this, the I.

Plunk. Here, in the hollow places.

The Frog fades into the sewage.

Gutterslut overlooks many sewage streams of the underworld, converging.

GUTTERSLUT

Yells.

Hello? Is anybody here?
Plunk, my ass.
I'm a scam, a stain. I am sacrilege,

I already know how it ends. Failure is my answer,
I'm fated to remain silent, a failure,
a thing that clogs the drain.

ENSEMBLE OF AFTERGLOW

Singing.

I want the memory of me to be a happy one.
I'd like to leave an afterglow of smiles when life is done.

RIDING SAYS HELLO FROM UNDERWATER

Static, or is it censorship of information? Do you see the Afterglow? Static, or murk, muffles Riding's voice on the other line. In the body of Grief, she swims.

A telephone unlike any telephones before appears. On a table? Floating midair? Is it buried? And if so, will Gutterslut put her ear to the ground to hear it ring? In doing so, what else does she hear? A pulse? A thump? A glint on a ripple? The quavering in Riding's voice? Or is it the onset of release?

RIDING

I—I thought I'd call
Static.
We still haven't found him, or his body.
It's almost as if he—
Static.
I always could imagine
the two of you—
staying together,
Static.

Who knows,
maybe he'll turn—
Static.
I'm swimming.
I bought a snorkel and—
Static.
To look under—
Static.

FROG
Walks across the stage, reading the Phaedo.
By not knowing where the body is, we think of it more as undying.
Looks out.
The outcomes multiply…

MOURNING MORE THAN A SINGULAR LOSS

Underwater. Inside a sunken dream of a kitchen, adorned with the familiar raspberry wallpaper, hanging pots and pans, etc. Shafts of light cut through the polluted atmosphere.

How does the Afterglow apparate, embodied? There is a You and there are the Yous you've passed through. How would we portray the parts discarded? The embodiments somnambulate on stage to assemble an ensemble—drifting slantwise, as long and looming as evening shadows.

FROG

Walks back across stage, reading the Phaedo.

The body, undying,

Looks out.

multiplies…

ENSEMBLE OF AFTERGLOW

Each one, another set of outcomes.
Another interpretation of loss, undefined.
Each embodies their result.

1. My loss is an ecdysiast, a contortionist circling sod to dirt in the front yard.
2. My loss is the Signified in a cold sweat, free from its Signifier for an afternoon, buying a six-pack.
3. Feigns self-containment, but is ruled by a planet characterized by rapid and unpredictable changeableness of mood.
4. A cache ultradeep, I frack, speculate finitude, regretregret, and my nearlynearly drains from my whole. Where does it go when it goes?
5. Coffee grounds at the bottom of the mug. A language built of resemblances, smiles familiar and weak, a palm-to-palm. I gently squeeze a hand attached to another body to appear more animate to myself. A cloud with ellipses hangs loose above our heads.
6. My loss appears as a pocket-sized reportage of Falcon 9, a sudden and distinct realization of—
7. There I was, gesturing again to the gold-green heap, when I see my loss, flashing above the water, a wave waving over the waves. Do I wave back?
8. I puncture a hole in my loss and breathe myself upright.

Repeat 2x; and—differently timed. The Afterglow will
read the manifestation of their loss once in lieu of movement.

GUTTERSLUT

Stands center stage with spotlight.

It's been how long, and no trace. No sign.
We've printed posters. So many have called
and believed they've seen him. But it's just
uncanny resemblance.   To be lost,
or in a state of loss, is revealed pervasive
in their passing expressions. We've spent how

long calling his name along the river.
We called his name along the river.

AFTERGLOW 1

We called his name along the river.

His face on the flyers resembled the others…

We received phone calls.
Yes, I saw him, they'd say.

AFTERGLOW 2

Walking down the highway.

Or, Yes. I saw him.

AFTERGLOW 3

He is in the granary.

I gave him a ride. Or,

Or,

Or, yes I think I saw—

I built a wall. I saw him—

AFTERGLOW 4

Yes, I saw her, years ago…
she told me she was lost, and
I closed my door.

AFTERGLOW 5

Yes, I saw him when I was a child.
She used to walk in the field
behind our house.

AFTERGLOW 6

He was crowded with himself, or
with many selves. He was fleeing.
I saw him.

Her. I saw them.

I saw all of him leave—

AFTERGLOW 2

En masse. I saw him and her.
I saw they. I saw them.

I saw them multiply in fog,

AFTERGLOW 7

Under the bridge. I saw

I saw all of him. I didn't stop. I didn't offer help. I saw him, and I drove by. As a kid I saw him and I was told *don't look him in the eye*.

AFTERGLOW 8

I was told *keep walking*. As a kid I saw him in the subway.

AFTERGLOW 8 & 1

En masse. I saw him and her.
I saw they. I saw them.

En masse. I saw him and her.
I saw they. I saw them

while walking at night,
along a fence.

AFTERGLOW 3

I saw them in exodus. I heard about him,
and the rest,

AFTERGLOW 4

In the papers.
Without papers.

in the papers.

Without papers.

AFTERGLOW 5

I heard they were turned away.

AFTERGLOW 6

I heard he mentioned an attack.

GUTTERSLUT

Don't shoot, he wrote on a slip of paper
the day before he went missing. I heard

AFTERGLOW 7

they were attacked.

He fled.

They fled.

AFTERGLOW 8

They've been fleeing. I heard about it in the news.

AFTERGLOW 1
I saw them pass on the bus.

AFTERGLOW 2
I saw them through the window,
looking out.

AFTERGLOW 3
I saw my reflection. Look—

GUTTERSLUT
Angry.
I turned away.

AFTERGLOW 4
I have always turned away. I heard—

AFTERGLOW 5
them! In the park
asking for—

AFTERGLOW 6 & 7
—a chorus of them, and I crossed the street.

Hands reach through the flesh, interweave.
Is to interweave a product of grief?

FROG

The family, once interwoven.

I, the product of the family

evacuated. I,

afterthought. I, hindsight.

I, so-called, composite, infectious

amalgamation of the "I"

themselves, sticky, plastic, plural.

AFTERGLOW

(Who believes in a we, a plural, now anyhow?)

FROG

Smelters, concentrators, processors

along the crick. Industrial

carrier, the river. The I. The ruckus

that hardly ensues, suchandsuch a shame.

Waterfunk. Watersludge.

AUTOPOIESIS

Gutterslut approaches two glints of Afterglow, embodied.

They dance the numbered section below. The dance is a trade-off, moving through and into one another's experience—never precisely. Each time the light shifts, one becomes the other, is absorbed and absorbs.

1. [Shifts in the light until...]
2. [Shifts in the light until...]
3. [Shifts in the light until...]
4. [Shifts in the light until...]
5. [Shifts in the light until...]
6. [Shifts in the light until...]
7. [Shifts in the light until...]

8. [Shifts in the light until…

until…

until…

Gutterslut is transported across a braiding of rivers and passes through channels until breaching—gasp!—above water in the River-That-Might-As-Well-Be. Gutterslut is whisked downstream through the heavy current until she sees a boat, grabs hold of its stern, and climbs on board. The boat doubles as a wheelchair. Maybe it is shown as a wheelchair with inflatable sides, cupholders, and a small umbrella.

GUTTERSLUT

I could hear you singing from across the river.

CHRIS

That bad, huh?

GUTTERSLUT

Have you seen anyone pass through?
Who appears lost?

CHRIS

Moss, gloss, Tabasco sauce.

GUTTERSLUT
You?

CHRIS
Who, me?

GUTTERSLUT
No, but I—I'm Gutterslut.

CHRIS
Alright, if you want to play like that,
my name is Chris. You can join me
if you'd like; have a seat. I'm singing
to my old love, I guess you could say.

GUTTERSLUT
Where are they now?

CHRIS

They are here, not physically, but as a fading
light, a gaze… passing by page by page. Look.

Grief is the afterlife, and another way to say
unaccepted outcomes. This is where we are,
amidst what can't be undone.

It's worth settling into…
get to know the others.
I myself haven't found
any other choice.

Both lean back, tired, as if pressed down by heat.

GUTTERSLUT

And your song?

CHRIS

Because silence is another kind of death—

But does true silence exist? As they quiet, a song begins to swell… the humming of the Frog? A fishing line tugging to signal a distant encounter? A high note, ringing? Or the light tempo of the respirator, a breath, the persistent, measured evidence of living despite the constant effort of it all. Or is it a reminder to breathe? Or, when at night, the respirator stops.

Gutterslut takes a sudden, sharp inhalation.

Lights off.

Appendix

The reference to the flooding of rivers as the imagination is credited to Toni Morrison, "The Site of Memory," published in *What Moves at the Margin: Selected Nonfiction* (University Press of Mississippi, 2008).

Mary Anna Evans wrote "Flushing the Toilet Has Never Been Riskier," published in *The Atlantic* in 2015, which is where I found quotes about the primary and secondary treatment of wastewater for the prologue.

The oil-slick Cuyahoga River has caught fire at least thirteen times from years of industrial waste and pollutants. A *Time* magazine article from 1969 wrote the Cuyahoga is the river that "oozes rather than flows" and in which a person "does not drown but decays." This partly inspired the River-That-Formerly-Was, as well as the term "hauntology" coined by Derrida. Here, the play is haunted by rivers, thruways, and lifelines that are no longer accessible.

I was intrigued by the dramaturgy of Ola Kraszpulska in "Visual Explorations of Metaphysical Ideas in the Works of Sarah Ruhl," from *Old Stories, New Readings: The Transformative Power of the American Drama* (Cambridge Scholars Publishing, 2015). I incorporated Kraszpulska's language (in her analysis of *Eurydice*): "So we may remember to forget."

I referenced Judith Butler in the prologue: "Part of the very problem of contemporary political life is that not everyone counts as a subject." This line is from the first chapter, "Precarious Life, Grievable Life," in *Frames of War* (Verso, 2009). Butler's description of "the speaking body" from *Excitable Speech: A Politics of the Performative*

(Routledge, 1997) was influential.

In Aldo Leopold's *Round River* (Oxford University Press, 1993), he writes, "One of the penalties of an ecological education is that one lives alone in a world of wounds," which I quote in the prologue. The final lines of the prologue are attributed to Samuel Taylor Coleridge, "The Rime of the Ancient Mariner." Coleridge was alluding to life at sea, but I use it to reference the (mis-)management of natural resources and lack of water in the world of this play.

The Fisherman says "A great wind carries me across the sky." This line is from an Ojibwe saying which is "Sometimes I go about in pity for myself, and all the while, a great wind carries me across the sky."

I heard the phrase, "Grief is the afterlife," in passing at the Thinking Its Presence conference at the Poetry Center in 2017. I never caught the name of the person who said this, but it succinctly captured my intentions for the world-building of the play.

After completing the play, I learned "Afterglow" is a title of a famous funereal poem by Helen Lowrie Marshall ("I'd like the memory of me to be a happy one. / I'd like to leave an echo whispering softly down the ways, / Of happy times and laughing times and bright and sunny days.")

Acknowledgments

Thank you, first and foremost, to Prageeta Sharma who inspired me to pursue performance texts and also reminded me that "grief is the worst club to be a part of." Thank you, Prageeta, for your encouragement, generosity, wisdom, and friendship.

Lauren Korn has been a pillar of strength and insight throughout the editorial process, and I can't imagine navigating it without her. Her attention to detail as a reader and editor, as well as peace of mind and uplifting perspective, has carried me at many points in time. Ken White has likewise been essential to the creation of this play through several major points. Not only has his own writing contributed to my understanding and appreciation of cross-genre texts, but he shared the resources and deep listening I needed to complete this project and embark on a lifetime of learning.

I also want to thank Kate Morris, who inducted me into the world of theatre and faithfully attended our weekly "Apocalypse Office Hours" at The Golden Rose to discuss love and dramaturgy with me. I assisted Between the Lines Theatre with the production of her play, IN THE SNOW, which premiered at The Roxy. It directly influenced my dramatic speech and use of audience interaction in this play, and Kate continues to teach me how to create theatre from the everyday. She is my co-conspirator.

This play began as a series of performances. The performances wouldn't have been possible without Mary Ann Bonjorni who challenged me to develop new ways of communicating and collaborating. I am immensely grateful for my friends in the journey: Erin Langley, Padyn Humble, Jon Green, Richie Masias, and Jasper Pelle for the unending laughter and ideas. Also, Logan Prichard shared his patience and humor during our brainstorming sessions when we thought we would co-produce this play; we never did (at least not yet), but he showed me how to imagine the text embodied, and kept my spirits high along the way. Alyssa Kennamer was also essential to the translation of poetry into a score for movement and was abundantly supportive of the project.

Thank you to my other friends and inspirations in Missoula: Katie Kane for your wicked genius and golden heart; Sherwin Bitsui for your expansive perspective; Larissa FastHorse for reminding me to lean into the vulnerability and endurance required to write; Maren Schiffer for your sweetness and observant critique; Carlos Medina for yelling at me on stage when I needed it most; Nora Saks and Rachel Smith for sharing a home with me through the hardest process of writing this play, and so many others.

It goes without saying that I couldn't have written this play without the love of my family. Thank you, Mom, Dad, Derek, Kyle, Mavis, and Nonee. I am so lucky to have you. Thank you for your acceptance of me, your faith, and for teaching me to follow my passions.

Of course, thank you to Noah's immediate family for welcoming me into your lives and seeing our love for one another. You are uniquely warm, caring, creative, and intelligent people and I feel so blessed to know you. Even with the distance, I feel close to you. Thank you for bringing Noah into the world. Noah, you showed me how to love and celebrate myself and all people. You are the brightest light. The world stopped existing without you in it, but we have found ways to keep living.

I learned with my friends how to really take care of others, and what interdependence feels like. I believe friendship is a radical practice for social change. I have found courage and trust in my friendships, and they've taught me how to be responsible to other people. Thank you, Tyler Pell, Piera Greathouse Cox, Brett Sisun, Dyllan Hersey, Cole Hersey, Claire Schechtman, Kelly Mehigan, Imogen Field, Mary Kate Moroney, Jack Washer, Marija Brzev, Will Mehigan, Campbell Steers, Anthony Rianda, Nico Liebman, and so many others. Shelby Meyers, if we hadn't traveled together around the South after Noah's memorial, and if I hadn't been graced with your calm groundedness and sense of wonder, then I don't think this play would exist. Special thanks to Clem Hepburn for everything you are and for teaching me that love requires action and intention.

I appreciate the editors at Tarpaulin Sky for shortlisting my manuscript, and referring me to my publisher, Tyler Crumrine. I feel so fortunate to work with you, Tyler. You pour your heart into Plays Inverse, which sustains an exceptional and vital constituent of contemporary writing. Thank you for your patience while bringing this book, and others, into the world amidst a pandemic (and more). I am immensely grateful for you and your faith in this work. I am honored to have the art of both Aiden Koch and Lauren Roche accompany this play, and admire them both immensely as creators.

Last but not least, thank you to the watershed in Western Oregon, the tribes native to this region, especially the Kalapuya whose ancestral homelands are in Eugene, OR, and the Water Protectors at Standing Rock Reservation who remind us that "water is life."

Jordan Chesnut is a poet and playwright.